MY MEGAVERSE IS CHRIST

a memoir that brought me closer to God

KABIR
"BIR WITNESS"
JAMAL

Trilogy Christian Publishers

A Wholly Owned Subsidary of Trinity Broadcasting Network

2442 Michelle Drive

Tustin, CA 92780

For information, address Trilogy Christian Publishing

Rights Department, 2442 Michelle Drive, Tustin, CA 92780.

Trilogy Christian Publishing/ TBN and colophon are trademarks of Trinity Broadcasting Network.

For information about special discounts for bulk purchases, please contact Trilogy Christian Publishing.

Trilogy Disclaimer: The views and content expressed in this book are those of the author and may not necessarily reflect the views and doctrine of Trilogy Christian Publishing or the Trinity Broadcasting Network.

10 9 8 7 6 5 4 3 2 1

Library of Congress Cataloging-in-Publication Data is available.

ISBN 979-8-89333-113-4

ISBN (ebook) 979-8-89333-114-1

DEDICATION

My wife has been encouraging me to finish this book ever since I started working on it. She is my peace and my best friend on many levels. I am extremely grateful to experience a love so strong, and blessed to make albums with her and be so creative together for a lifetime. It's not just music; our married life is full of love and creativity. I'm fully supportive of her because we are one and share a quality of Jesus, with unconditional love for each other and creation. She not only has a major impact on my life, but she will also have a major impact on the world. A special recognition to my stepdaughters: your love played a major role in my healing process and my heart is postured to continue loving you in a mighty way! To my grand-daughter: you give me so much joy and purpose! Grandpa loves you unconditionally.

FOREWORD

When Kabir and his wife Jocelyn walked into our living room on that cold January morning of 2023, I had no idea just how much all our lives would change in one short year.

In early 2020, the Lord had made a radical shift in my and my husband's lives. The previous 18 years had seen us opening our home to countless individuals who were deep in the throes of addiction and had no way out. Those were tough years, raising our four young children in a home packed with people with major criminal backgrounds, all out of our love for Jesus. Many of those who came through the home experienced the love and freedom of Christ and have been "adopted" into our family. In those days, here in New Hampshire, the opiate crisis was at a peak, and our home was capturing and bringing healing to the heartache associated with it all, firsthand.

In early 2020 we had an experience at our church gathering that shook us to the core. A young woman, medically diagnosed with mental health issues and demonically influenced, began acting out and demonically manifesting in the midst of our meeting. As church leaders, we rose to the occasion by commanding evil influencesto leave, praying for the young woman, declaring freedom and healing over her. But after four hours of contending for this woman, she left still bound. It was a confusing and heartbreaking time for us, as we called God's goodness and power into question on issues surrounding what the world describes as severe mental illness.

Where was He? Why hadn't He answered our cries? How come we were not able to walk in the power and authority described in Scripture? How come that woman was unable to get free? Over the course of the next several years, the Lord thoroughly answered these questions and more. He adjusted our foundation to be one that was immoveable, and He revealed His truth, power, and authority on issues regarding mental health and its deep ties to spirituality.

From the fall of 2020 to spring of 2021 our home saw a transition from helping those coming out of addiction to bringing freedom to those who were bound in their minds and in their behaviors. The Lord brought us people who were bound by trauma, fear, anxiety, depression, schizophrenia, etc. As we were seeing across the state and the world the numbers of mental health patients rise dramatically, in our home we were seeing people getting fully set free and healed by the gift of salvation that is offered through Jesus Christ. Our eyes became open to a much bigger battle over the hearts and minds of humanity than we had ever been previously. aware of. And we saw that when engaged in a head-to-head battle, Jesus wins.

In December of 2022 I had received a phone call from a good friend and sister in Christ, Jocelyn, about some things that were going on with her newlywed husband Kabir. He had been diagnosed with mental illness at a very young age, in and out of mental hospitals, and here he was at 37 years old fighting the biggest battle of his life. We told them to come. Kabir entered the room, a towering presence over his tiny but fiery wife. His hands were shaking incessantly, not from fear but from the extremely high dosages of the 14 different medications he was on. He couldn't pick up a cup or hold a pencil. But his smile lit up the room. Jocelyn took the floor, speaking the truth of the power of God. She had heard what God was doing at our house, and she had faith in 100% freedom for her husband. On that day we committed to a journey with these friends, now turned family. Kabir would be free once and for all of this diagnosis, of all the spiritual influences that were plaguing him, and of all the medications that were in his body. As I am writing this, we are just passing the one-year anniversary of that first meeting. And Kabir? He is no longer shaking, he is off of

ALL but two small doses of medication (with plans to be fully off everything soon). He does not have manic episodes or uncontrollable behaviors anymore. He is not a slave to racing thoughts or things of his past anymore. With the help of his wife and our church family, he has planted his feet firmly on the foundation of the salvation that was given to him through Christ Jesus. And no wind or storm will ever be able to make this house fall down again.

Kabir speaks in his book about staying true to who you are, in life, in lyrics, in relationships, etc. And he speaks that from experience. On his journey, through the rises and falls, the Lord has faithfully been stripping away everything that is not the true design that He had intended when He dreamed up Kabir. Everything that the world has tried to place on him or fashion him to fit just never seemed to feel right. And that is because it wasn't His design.

Nowadays as we sit in our home with the church in our Friday night meeting, guitars and djembes going, each one worshipping in their own words, it is not uncommon for Kabir to begin to rap out praise to God for all that He has done, and all that God has brought him through. This man was made for worship, whether through music or writing. His creativity is astounding. And he has the experience to back up all that he is saying. His heart is truly for others to succeed.

And so, I encourage you, listen to what he tells you. Listen to it in this book, listen to it on Spotify or YouTube or anywhere else his songs are played. He is speaking a message. And that message can change your life.

Lydia O'Leary

PREFACE

I prayed for the spirit of wisdom, understanding, and clarity when writing this book, *My Megaverse is Christ*, and I share my journey with you throughout these pages so you can see what I see. I have been through so much in the music field and I'm going to help you on your journey to success by letting Jesus work on you the same way He worked on me to be who I am today. I will cover everything you need to know to make a career for yourself independently and succeed with a strong work ethic, first and foremost putting God in the forefront. We should all be Holy Spirit-led in all decisions in life, and a big goal of mine is to love on others and spread the gospel in my music, set the tone to evangelize the industry, and bring artists, producers, engineers, and executives to Christ. Time for change. This book will give you the purpose to pray for yourself and others, be more confident, and have more faith in all matters in life while pursuing a music career.

ACKNOWLEDGEMENTS

The unconditional love of Pastor Lydia and my Church of Believers.

INTRODUCTION

My father always told me, "Keep doing what you're doing, Kabir!" I get emotional because he was sick, and he really motivated me to pursue a career in music before he passed away in December 2009. I love my father and I love God's plan in my life, because losing my dad brought me to the realization that I needed to establish a deeper connection with God. I write music for myself and others, I produce, engineer, and run a successful music ministry with my wife. This book is not only about my experience but the knowledge of the music business from industry professionals I've built business relationships with over my many years in the industry. I've been getting recognition for the past eighteen years, mainstream radio, major hip hop blogs, producer credits for major labels, and many licensing deals with TV placements. I've performed live shows consistently since 2009 and have even been booked in New York City. My name most are familiar with in the music industry is Bir Witness. I am here to help you achieve success through accepting Jesus into your heart, reading and learning about my life and journey of ups and downs personally and professionally, and always keeping God first. I will tell you like my father told me, "Keep doing what you're doing," in your case by reading this book!

Kabir "Bir Witness" Jamal

TABLE OF CONTENTS

1. GENESIS 21

2. BOSTON. 27

3. DANGER ZONE 29

4. PRAYING FOR SUCCESS 31

5. A SACRIFICE THAT CHANGED THE WORLD. 33

6. DAY ONE 35

7. PORTER STREET 39

8. BORN SINNER 41

9. DON'T BELIEVE THE HYPE .43

10. DON'T BITE THE HAND THAT FEEDS YOU 45

11. JEWELS AND GEMS 49

12. ALL THINGS JESUS 51

13. MY HIP HOP BEGINNINGS. 53

14. EXECUTIVE PRODUCER. 57

15. CHRISTIAN HIP HOP 61

16. STRUGGLES TO SUCCESS .65

17. SHADY BUSINESS 69

18. PRACTICE MAKES PERFECT 71

19. WHAT'S YOUR SOUND 77

20. SONG STRUCTURE 81

21. SONG WRITING 83

22. GET A GREAT ENGINEER .85

23. THE MIXTAPE 89

24. STAY ACTIVE ON SOCIAL
    MEDIA AND INVEST 91

25. RADIO PLAY AND STREAMING YOUR MUSIC . . .93

26. MUSIC STREAMING 95

27. MAJOR HIP HOP BLOGS 97

28. BE A VISUAL ARTIST 99

29. CHRIST VISION TV IS THE FUTURE 101

30. MAKING AN ALBUM 103

31. ALBUM ARTWORK 113

32. MERCHANDISE 117

33. HAVING A MANAGER. 119

34. PERFORMING AN ALBUM LIVE. 123

35. LICENSING DEALS AND ROYALTY CHECKS . . .127

36. ALBUM DISTRIBUTION AND RECORD DEALS. .129

37. ABOUT KABIR "BIR WITNESS" JAMAL 131

"So, GOD created Man in his own image, in the image of GOD he created him. Male and female, he created them." Genesis 1:27

THE GENESIS

I started out songwriting, recording, engineering, producing, and helping others share their testimony since the age of fifteen. As a writer, I have been weaving my story together for years, making good progress in my journey. Everything happens for a reason, and I changed a lot throughout the years. I can't say it enough. I'm married to the love of my life, Jocelyn Jamal, and Jocelyn was blessed with the gift of rhymes. She is perfect for me, and I am grateful for a wife with a passion for music, compassion for struggling souls, and a mind focused on Christ. The story of Adam and Eve is not our story but a biblical one to pull from. Our genesis in this lifetime is my wife telling me to bite into the Tree of Life and live forever. She gets it!! We're more like Ruth and Boaz in the Bible, because we were made for each other. She protects our crops, and I will always protect her in spirit, the best way I can with GOD armor.

 A kid I went to high school with was a rapper and he encouraged me to be one too. I was fascinated by his label and the Boston sound. I wrote my first rhyme and he loved it! He told me I was a battle rapper. From there I was motivated and wanted to rap battle everyone and I did. I even rap battled the Porter Street Gang, and they realized I had courage, even though I didn't win. I remember one gang member said I'll twist your top off and Kabir you and I was fascinated by his metaphor. When I rap battled in school, I loved how the high school crowd reacted when I said a great punchline and right then and there I fell in love with man's approval. It wasn't until I started doing music for Jesus that I knew my identity in all things, not just hip hop, because it definitely made me a way better person and rapper. I encourage you to turn your life to Jesus and fill your life with the Holy Spirit. My megaverse is Christ. He is the King of all kings.

Before I became a battle rapper, I battled depression, and I remember the moment I struck my head with a kitchen knife. Jesus came to my rescue. I ran away from home; I was twelve and in this very moment I realized I was blessed with life and had a better understanding of right and wrong. When I returned home, I suffered depression from running away. When I realized I was forgiven, I felt on top of the world and was diagnosed with bipolar disorder. I blamed myself for everything growing up; even went crazy being a Muslim during 9/11. I felt responsible and became suicidal about it and told my dad I wanted to jump out my upstairs window. I was hospitalized and overmedicated from that innocent.

When I fully understood and accepted Jesus into my heart at thirty-four years old, He visited me. I was taking fourteen medications, and while I was watching YouTube He spoke life into me. He told me he loved my personality and after many months of studying the Bible Jesus revealed to me I made progress because I'm obedient with strong faith and obey whenever I'm moved by the depths of God's spirit. He gave me salvation and ultimately freedom, and all symptoms of bipolar and schizophrenia disappeared. This book is for every person I met in the mental hospitals I was admitted to since I was a kid, teenager, young adult in my twenties, and even as an adult while shaping this book. We all deserve freedom, and I will always speak life into you. You're stronger than you think. I remember the ones that found healing in my rhymes about feeling symptoms of mental health that didn't belong to me or them. It makes me a better artist, from struggle to success, from dark to light, from false-hood to Christ Himself.

We are one, and I will always spread the gospel across the world as an evangelist for everyone who needs to hear "Jesus loves you." That's it, Jesus loves you unconditionally; in whatever condition you are in He loves you. You will be healed.

Music played a major role in the hospital, with us all watching music videos and listening to the radio. I know for certain my new music will give people—young,

, middle aged, and older—the strength, understanding, wisdom, and clarity to do what I did to stop the madness. I would always study what I was going through mentally and emotionally. I've been broken for too long, and it's about time I was fixed in Jesus' mighty name. I'm a survivor of schizophrenia and severe bipolar disorder. The cure is Jesus. Whenever I put my complete faith in Christ, He blows my mind with the peace He has given me, coming off my high doses of fourteen medications. My past does not define me. I am a new creation and a witness to Christ's miracle of being reborn and covered in His precious blood and a reconstructed heart, mind, and spirit after baptism in purity with the Holy Spirit.

I felt suicidal going off my medication, and I gave it to Jesus. I experienced extreme racing thoughts, and I gave it to Jesus. I was irritated by a lowering of medication, and I gave it to Jesus. My testimony is establishing a better relationship with Father God through Jesus and surrendering everything to His will, and I went through that and trusted the process of healing from gang activity, falsehood, schizophrenia, and severe bipolar. I serve an awesome God, and my relationship with my Father in heaven is now stronger and more present in my heart, mind, and spirit.

I have so many stories of being under the influence of gangs, drug dealing, fourteen psych ward visits, many ICU visits, court cases, probation, and feeling hopeless and broke. I am not currently suffering from mental health issues. I have the mind of Christ, and my megaverse is His scripture. I follow better with time as an obedient soldier of Christ. God is real; give your life to Him and make music for His Kingdom for the hearts of your brothers and sisters in Christ.

I started with battle rap and wanted the approval of man for two decades, then made a sacrifice for myself and ultimately my family and here I am, a man of faith-fulness. I'm a stepfather to two beautiful young women and grandfather to my amazing granddaughter Zyralise. I'm married to my best friend Jocelyn. We have a Christian hip hop label, and we work with other Christian artists in the kingdom; you should follow suit. Jesus loves you. and your megaverse is Christ. You just have to give your life to Him and make better music with the Holy Spirit.

BOSTON

I was born in Boston and raised the first six years of my life in the heart of the city Roxbury. I remember Alpine Street and visiting my grandmother constantly on Circuit Street. My nana is my second mom and I miss her so much. She wanted to see me in concert at 89 years old; she had style and grace and she told me to marry a Puerto Rican woman and I did!!! I was a city kid and then we moved to a Jewish town called Sharon and I told Boston I'd be right back!!! Sharon was dope; my dad moved us to a great life. We felt rich; we were well taken care of and I was extremely busy as an elementary school kid. I worked for my dad before I got to middle school and I hated it, sweeping, cleaning, rolling out big rugs for the Muslims to pray on. I remember my favorite rapper was Will Smith and the song "Wild, Wild West." My older brother bought me the CD for my birthday. Our rooms had no doors, so I was always hearing the 90s hip hop blasting out his speakers, but I wasn't intrigued to try out writing until we moved to a town called Stoughton and I met the rapper I spoke of in The Genesis.

DANGER ZONE

I was walking on the highway, cars racing past, trucks beeping their horns and swerving away from my suicidal self. I was lost in the city, and I honestly forgot how I ended up in Boston around the homeless. "You have a good head on your shoulders," said the poor old man. "Go home," said another. Instead, I treated myself like I did not have a house in the suburbs. I ran away from my parents and wanted freedom on these streets. I lost touch with reality when I went off my many medications at the time and found false identity in

bipolar diagnosis. I just wanted to be safe, and this diagnosis put my life in danger many times.

I survived, and I looked very homeless when I found my father's cousin's house. As I rang the doorbell, my father's aunt was surprised; she let me inside and called my parents as I cried for forgiveness. I have experienced a lot in life, and my mind loves field trips (well, not all of them). So it is time to go to the mental hospital, get out and write about it, but first catch up on my tenth-grade schoolwork before I record my next mixtape with my friends. I am a survivor of mental health, and my testimony will shock many. You see, I am writing a book on music, and I want you to understand what I have been through so far in my thirty-eight years and where I am now mentally. I am strong as an ox. It was not always like this, until I realized everything around me is Christ.

PRAYING FOR SUCCESS

When a well-known Compton producer was working on the motion picture album for his movie, I was doing business with a producer signed to him for many years. He is a man with strong faith and a great producer. He says sound without focus is just noise. He invited me to work with him in the studio because he saw my potential. We definitely have our ups and downs, but we have a solid connection in God. I prayed for him and the major label he's signed to. He really appreciated it. I brought a beat for 1K around the time the motion picture he produced music for was about to hit theaters and I am proud to say it was worth it. He produced my second album and many others. I did not know he was planting seeds of being married, having a family, making music with integrity, purpose, and respect. I always gravitated towards him and his producing and mixing. I even interviewed him when he left hip hop for good. We have been building for fourteen years. Last time we spoke, he was impressed with the business I did with a legendary rapper from New York and my connection to my engineer you will read more about in this book. I know a lot of people in the music business, but that means nothing when it comes to my relationship with the Father, the Son, and the Holy Spirit.

A SACRIFICE THAT CHANGED THE WORLD

GOD sacrifices His love to everyone and everything every day, to make sure this world is a better place. He shows up and gives His love when we are going through our worst. He even pulls love out of us and we grow. He even makes uncomfortable situations   feel comfortable, like when I hear GOD-driven music it does something to me. Even when a gangster gospel rap artist mentions GOD in his testimony I can relate to the feeling of struggle, being alone, having no one to talk to but GOD, and giving praise. I have felt compelled to help individuals through CHRIST, and I learned valuable lessons being left broken, broke, and homeless; what I learned was worth more than money. For awhile I was going house to house but could not find a home, because I had a homeless mentality. My father lifted me up and put me down so much I did not feel at home. I felt homeless and unbalanced before the diagnosis; others have done the same, but I know JESUS is my true home. Overall, as a grown man and looking back, he was a great father and I forgive him for his flaws as a parent of mine. Both my parents always had more to offer me than I could ever offer them, and I honor them daily. I was seeking for JESUS, and I came to the altar many times. I just couldn't stay in a peaceful place mentally without searching for it on the outside, through acceptance, popularity in music, a whole lot of shady business dreams and dealings on my way to JESUS I had a depression mentality and thought I needed medication to be well, but all I needed was CHRIST and a CHRIST connection with others.

DAY ONE

"When the seventh month came, and the children of Israel were in the towns, the people gathered as ONE MAN to Jerusalem." Ezra 2:1

Characters in my life reminded me of my parents, my brothers in a gang, just about anyone you could think of I've come across in life and pledged loyalty to. I was always reading so much Bible scripture about these characters and now really seeing my purpose and why my journey doing music professionally is so important to you, the reader. Helping people because they were broken was a full-time role of mine. I wanted people to understand them like I did, but they didn't want to sacrifice themselves for their calling and true purpose, truth, and understanding of what we were creating. They were shady in their ways, and it's understood why because they wanted to be a part of the shady business and admired those artists who glorify the success, not the work. I sacrificed myself for many, so getting to know Jesus I fell in love with His ultimate sacrifice for all our sins. Always knew who in music was Christian and even started listening to Christian songs more often than the shady business catalog nowadays. As a disciple of Jesus the Most High,

I believe Jesus is represented in so many obedient Christians; we are one with each other. I was exposed to this truth early but didn't know my identity was Jesus because I was raised to believe something else.

As a child of GOD, my gift of music and leadership will help you identify yourself, because when you surrender to His will and everything He has for you, your eyes will have CHRIST Vision and you will succeed. Welcome to my world and prepare to hear people who identify with success speak highly of me and my skills on the mic. GOD is very alive within me. Understand the gift, where it came from, and most importantly be grateful every day by putting Father GOD first.

We'll explore every aspect of the creative process and the music business. You can be a great songwriter for the world and an even better songwriter for the Kingdom of GOD. My day one at church recognized the JESUS in me. We saw each other as brothers and longtime friends, and I had just met him and his wife that day. I felt the creative power of GOD, And it was an experience JESUS did not want me to forget. The church celebrated a highly respected woman of GOD, and I ran into my day one again that had the same familiarity of my best friend I grew up doing music with. His upbringing was the Indian tradition of a guru like me, and he was grateful GOD brought him to JESUS just like me. He even had a Hindi name just like me. He described our connection as very CHRISTlike and I was in awe he saw so much JESUS that day as we crossed paths again. He looked impressed by something more intriguing than I realized. All glory to Lord Jesus for forgiving me when I couldn't even forgive myself.

Many friends in high school had a lower frequency but thought highly of me musically because I operated from a higher frequency. So, I took a risk and recorded them in my basement and considered this my beginning of everything in music and seeing things different. Looking at the whole view, my day one brought me to my brothers in the gang I had since moved on from because something more consistent was needed than death and jail. I'm always after peace and love and all my brothers love me for my kind spirit and loyalty to honor our day one; we started together in high school. Honestly, I never wanted to be beat up, stabbed, or shot so I was loyal and there was plenty of love there in a street corner type of way. It's all good.

My deepest connection came at thirty-four. I married a woman that shows me everything at once and she is my everything at once. I'm grateful for a royal family and an important role in a real family environment I absolutely fell in love with.

PORTER STREET

The positive lesson learned from the Porter Street Gang was oneness. We worked on music together as a team and my friend at the time motivated me to mix all the vocals on the spot. Everyone had different styles and flow, so the mixing was different volumes and effects depending on who was rapping their song lyrics. We made it work, and it also helped me develop an ear for mixing and overall sound. I'm a living, breathing record label because I have been the next level for so many in music just like a record label. My friends fresh out of jail, my friends struggling have all benefited from what I've solely done for myself first. Helping others is why I wrote this book. Since my teenage years, I have always wanted to help others shine and succeed greatly and live their dreams. Creatively, I am at the next level. You can ask the friends I recorded at fifteen or artists and producers I started with in the music industry. I'm known to bring the best out of people.

BORN SINNER

*"So whoever knows the right thing to do and
fails to do it, for him it is sin." James 4:17*

A lot of artists know better and sin like it's okay. I'd
probably be signed to a major record label if they didn't
know my identity is Christ. Never been a follower of
any demonic entity in the music business; yes, I did sign
a deal with a gangster rap label but he was a real one, a
famous rapper from Orange County, California. Hip hop
culture has poisoned so many and resulted in a type of
freedom GOD doesn't approve of. That is not freedom,
because they are still slaves, self-expression in a way
where you are led by evil. We are spiritual beings, and we
must not give in to the temptation of the enemy. Reaching
GOD realization is so foreign to people; they think a trip
to another country is the peace of mind they are looking
for. That didn't make the difference for me when I trav-
eled to India. My identity was always in

Jesus. I was just too blind to see it and too deaf to
hear it and way too dumb to understand CHRIST. Now
you understand my purpose and realize I have already
won, because me and JESUS are already one and it's my

mission to only serve the Kingdom of GOD and never poison the listener or reader. We are out here saving souls, not destroying them. We are all children of the living GOD JESUS CHRIST.

> *"So, faith comes from hearing, and hearing through the word of Christ." Romans 10:17*

DONT BELIEVE THE HYPE

"For GOD so loved the world, that he gave his only Son, that whoever believes in him should not perish but have eternal life." John 3:16

GOD is real and He loves you. I'm not impressed by the enemy's tactics to brainwash us and feed us rotten fruit. The Tree of Life is more rewarding.

than listening to the serpent like Eve did in the scripture. GOD wants us to spread the Gospel and do for ourselves in His Kingdom, not depend on wolves in sheep's clothing spreading falsehoods specifically aimed at weakness and not strength. Be the difference in this world and obey and praise GOD. Give your all to JESUS and spread the Good News!!!!

"You were unmindful of the Rock that bore you, and you forgot the GOD that gave you birth." Deuteronomy 32:18

DONT BITE THE HAND THAT FEEDS YOU

They wanted success but did not want to sacrifice what it took for success. Jesus walked the earth and sacrificed Himself daily spreading the gospel, healing the sick and suffering, while changing the world we live in with grace, compassion, love, and mercy, eventually leading up to His sacrifice of forgiveness of all sins for our freedom today.

I recorded two artists who understood the work and they signed a recording contract. They know pain and record best with a narrative of pain as a suffering child of God, of misfortune. He spoke about investing in yourself in this book and he sets the standard for doing so. I produced a record for his major label debut. He stays in touch and gives me credit for his humble beginnings. I recorded him for ten hours straight because he was so good at a young age, and I always wanted to see him win. We definitely pushed each other to a level we didn't know we could experience. We created a whole mixtape in a day, and we didn't stop for breaks. I was in control of the boards, and he was so on point and sounded incredibly confident and good on the mic. He had a good crew like I did when I was younger, so I was familiar with him, and I did not overthink; we just executed. He's an incredible talent who sacrificed himself to get to the top. He raps from experience, and I always text him scripture and discuss Christ on the phone. I'm just planting seeds so he can open the Bible and see everything for what it is for himself.

I believe in everyone, and I'll hang with you until you start putting rope around your neck. So many have taken my kindness for weakness, and I ask my Father to forgive them, because it's hard for me sometimes. I nailed so much to the cross and my emotions ran through me like vehicles on the highway, some big, some small exits on my way up. I'm already home. I'm just experiencing a return trip of sacrifice in purity and love of Jesus. I walk with the Lord as an evangelist bringing others to Christ and I'm already doing it through this book and simply walking outside telling homeless people "Jesus loves you!"

It's disappointing there are so many crabs in a barrel just pulling each other down, because they need to work through what I was free of. I've been through more gangster, crazier, no like crazy enough to be down with the Insane Gangster Disciples in Brockton, Massachusetts. I had to get that mentally stable and never got redeemed back to Good and I mean all the way good until I was baptized and gave my life to JESUS. I was literally out of my mind on those streets. I was trying to bring the homies to church but still was battling demonic forces myself. Gang members kept telling me they don't believe in God and I don't belong around here, so I left the many trap houses I entered for my salvation in Gangster Paradise. Sounds crazy, right?! That was my comfort zone.

Many stories come to mind, and I'm definitely a prayer warrior so I pray about everything! I don't miss the days I was dancing with the devil and always comfortable in the fire of Brockton, Massachusetts. I C-walked on the top of a Brockton Police vehicle as a vessel for Lucifer. I am not a gang member; I'm a child of GOD and I'm covered in the blood of Jesus. My vision is Christ, so I see everything differently. I'm different, always have been; my early producer told me to embrace it and take my music to the next level. He's my day one producer and a good friend from my past. I love my brother and I'm proud of his success in the music business. I have so much success as a producer he reached out to me about my work, and I saw his plaques with major contributions on FaceTime. We started from scratch together and built our own companies respectively, but my priority is having the reward of Christ and I have many plaques.

JEWELS & GEMS

I would have never imagined I would be the one that others respected, admired for my skills, songwriting ability, and performing because I never pictured myself being a successful, independent artist. I was always influenced by the local Boston scene of hip hop. It's funny, but now I can definitely show you full circle, how to succeed and keep winning without a major record deal, because that is exactly what I did through Jesus. I brought my A-game into this hip hop music world, and it has been recognized and paid attention to since I started. I hope my faith, experience, truth, and wisdom will help you to develop more confidence, creative inspiration, and even help you avoid the shady business of hip hop I experienced dealing with hip hop heavyweights.

So, what I'm going to do in this book is share with you the love of Jesus, lessons to develop your rap skills, creative development, the money business, and more importantly, a big takeaway would be some life lessons. What took me 20 years may save you some precious time after reading this book. Even with all of it, my biggest advice is to read Bible scripture, learn about Jesus, also learn from your mistakes and don't repeat them. I can't do it for you, it's your journey, but I will help guide you on the right path that I truly love: GOD-driven music and the people who I met along the way to salvation. In the end, it's up to you to discover your creative power within. Still, I learn from my experience, from me getting it right, making mistakes, dealing with mental health setbacks, and getting in my own way to reaching new heights through Christ. First things first, we'll pray, plan, execute and see it finished before we're done.

On a more practical level, I will introduce you to my producers, engineers, directors, graphic designers, and vital people in the music business you may want to get to know. You can always reach out to me find out their names and contact information.

You can contact me directly through my business email to really get plugged In. Here, Christvision1111@gmail.com. I'm here for your journey, the same way you discovered my book and showed up for mine. You were meant to find it. I want to see you win and unlock your creative power, to develop smart moves and get a better understanding of yourself along the way. We're all full of music and heaven will play the greatest tunes, so make sure your music is for the Lord so you can get on His playlist, the Greatest Playlist Ever.

ALL THINGS JESUS

"Streets and hip hop always went hand and hand…
a lot of your most successful hip hop labels were started
by gangsters and drug money. But back in the golden
era of hip hop, it was more about raising the conscious
mind and being street reporters from the hood. You would
rarely hear of artists turned celebrities killing each other
over colors in the music industry, back in those days. But
ever since the internet surfaced, the climate of gang banging has increased in hip hop in the last 10 years, causing
more rappers to have beefs with each other, even result-
ing in death. It is very unfortunate to see artists get killed,
and so many others that come from a gang bang culture
to hip Hop. Hopefully soon, brothers can come together
on a positive note, to change the narrative when it comes
to gang banging in hip hop. Bottom line, we must learn
to separate the streets from the music business and take a
more peaceful approach in today's hip hop." – My famous uncle in California

I'm from the East Coast and gang banging is active,
but what's more active is joining a church, healing the
sick, being a good human being, a having heart like Jesus.
Some of the biggest rappers are on the West Coast and

they are active Bloods and Crips. Hip hop gang culture started on the West Coast, but now it's everywhere! It's in the US and it's global. I've done business with a famous West Coast Crip like my legendary uncle. We consider each other family; I have prayed for him, and he loves my music! He's been solid for over a decade, always supporting the past and present Bir Witness. I was having a jam session with my granddaughter when he called and let me know he does everything for his family when I mentioned I was blasting my album *KING OF KINGS*. Long Beach, California's Own was a lesson learned, and the famous Blood from Compton really put me on. I even signed a deal with a label named after a Gangsta Disciple, Hitman Crew in Chicago. The label is a positive way to represent the owner's family through dominating with music, not violence. He was always supportive and respectful when I was there and also when I left. I was once told you must choose a side to be a rapper but that's not true. All you have to do is be yourself. Period. My big homie once said he didn't have many choices. But YOU do. He told me gang culture and hip hop (where he was from in Cali) go hand in hand because he was raised off early West Coast music. They were not break-dancing out West, they were all gang-affiliated, doing their dirt, and that's what made music because it was their reality, during that time.

MY HIP HOP BEGINNINGS

My father always told me "I know you better than you know yourself, boy," and I believed him. One thing was for sure, he really did believe in me more than I believed in myself, in many things, due to his wisdom. He believed in me, and it took him passing away for me to begin to believe in myself spiritually, creatively, mentally, and to spread my wings and fly.

Before I was able to see what he'd seen in me, I always wanted to sound like my neighborhood friends growing up. I sounded goofy because I wasn't being myself. A few years passed, and all the fun I was having at fifteen years old turned into being heavily influenced by gang culture, and I wasn't even familiar with it on a personal level; I just knew I wanted to be down. I admired how everybody would rap and I liked the brotherhood, but it turned into a nightmare.

I boxed one of my neighborhood friends. I started doing music around sixteen and I was beating him up then. From every corner I was getting hit by the other homies from the gang; after a bloody nose, lip, and just a beat down I was down, and nothing was ever the same from this experience. After weeks of not being myself and songwriting from a twisted perspective, I found a way out of Porter Street, the street this all took place on. I experienced salvation from gangs recently after several encounters with Jesus' voice and presence. I even wrote music about it on my album *BROKEN SILENCE* and disc two *SAVED BY CHRIST*. Around that time I left Porter Street. I was still young, so I chose to stay close to my father after feeling freedom from gangs. I wrote some of my dopest songs in his presence. I went into a higher frequency creative zone when my father was close in proximity. After his funeral. I had to learn how to believe in myself and I realized that I didn't have my father, but I did have GOD, the Father; you just have to believe in Him. Strengthen your worship, keep GOD first and you will experience stronger faith.

2010 is when my unique writing of lyrics began, and I realized I was sharper with my songwriting skills because I was just being myself. So, before you start getting all excited about your music and you want to sound like everyone else, step back and remember to be yourself. Bring this book to every studio session and stay focused, because a lot of time can be wasted and if you are not directed in a positive way, you can lose yourself. I'm not

just successful because I rap good, I'm successful because I put God first. The Lord opens doors for you when
you remember Him. He's the real Executive Producer.
The devil is a liar, and the devil is shady business.

> *"Being an Executive Producer is a mysteriously*
> *important role for any thriving project. Long*
> *hours and bouts with creativity is all too much*
> *a part of the process and so are the uncreative*
> *aspects. Nevertheless, the end product is always*
> *rewarding no matter how many times you have*
> *to start over."*
>
> *– My mentor in Los Angeles, California*

 EXECUTIVE PRODUCER

My first professional experience with executive producing was creating a short album at a luxury studio in Boston. My older brother introduced me to this studio. Even at the age of twenty, I had passion and creative ideas. It seemed natural for me. I would bring concepts, stories, hooks, and some great production to the sessions. The engineer was very creative, and my older brother who sang the hooks and was featured on the album, and others since, made my songs even better. In later years I returned the favor to him, with top notch verses and even introduced him to a couple engineers that he did great work with.

When I finished the short album, I needed to develop a name for myself that was an expression of this album, so while speaking with my family, I came up with my rap name "Bear" Witness. This was a name that I thought was appropriate to how I witnessed my life and observed the things around me. My mother suggested I should spell it, "B-I-R" Witness like my name. That's how God's grace works, because this name was perfect. You probably have your story for your name in hip hop also. I realize now that I chose a rap name that would gain popularity, garner respect, and have a consistent fan base for the next sixteen years and counting. So, choose what you want to call yourself and how others address you.

I fell in love with executive producing, and that's when I met my friend, a producer from Weymouth, Massachusetts. He and I created my first album, *Perfection,* and had a productive work schedule for years. A favorite engineer and producer of mine is a

person I call a mentor and friend from Flint, Michigan. This dude can really mix a record, and I know it has to do with his executive producing skills. He hears the mix finished before anyone else does and so do I. An executive producer should always add elements that compliment the artist to a song or an entire project. We created the greatest unreleased album ever and you will never hear it. He said to me, "What about all the work you put n?" When I explained I was a Christian now and was getting married, he said, "Witness, what about all the work I did?"

"Sorry, bro, no longer chasing the world," I said. "I'm currently working with an executive producer in Las Vegas, Nevada and we are a hit factory with Christian hip hop." He picks the best beats off our conversations and prayers. He edits and arranges music to stand out with clarity to the listener. I'm grateful for this opportunity to work with a professional of my same faith. We have a Christ connection, and you can hear it and see it in the music we're putting out. What would have taken thousands of dollars my brother in Christ provided, resources that helped push everything forward for close to nothing. God's plans in motion.

CHRISTIAN HIP HOP

Being a Christian or gospel musician entails more than meets the eye. I must not only ensure that my heart and actions are pure, but I must also watch out that I am not leading anyone astray. Not just picking a beat and writing a song will do; I must also pray about it and ask God to guide me and reveal the message He wants to convey. I must move aside and out of the way.

When ministering through music, there are many misconceptions. My acts, conduct, and even how I respond to challenges in life should all reflect a life of righteousness. Never will I profess to be perfect, and I never will be. Like everyone else, I am in desperate need of Yeshua. It doesn't matter what rank one holds, how long someone has been saved, or even if they are still in the dark. Since I am no better than anyone else, I must not be arrogant. When choosing an instrumental, I must follow the spirit's guidance. I occasionally find myself crafting a song to a beat that may be uncomfortable for me. However, the message that is conveyed makes everything seem to always go together seamlessly. Before writing, recording, or even listening to an instrumental, I must always take a moment to pray. I also need to ask God to slay my flesh so that His will, not mine, can prevail.

Due to the darkness, I was exposed to and the associated memories, I might not always enjoy referencing my history in my music. However, there is a purpose for bringing up all the anguish and pain; it can be a support to someone who is hurting at the time or to encourage someone by letting them know they are not alone.

It may be perfect timing for them, because if I can be delivered out of the hell that I was in at one point in time, anyone can do it. This song is more than just music; it's about sowing seeds, saving souls, sharing the great commission, and demonstrating the love of the Almighty Lord.

"Hip hop and music saved my life. My father, mother, and my elders have contributed great wisdom and faith towards my creativity, so how can I fail when grace always picks me back up and makes me better and better?"

- **Bir Witness**

STRUGGLES TO SUCCESS

While writing this chapter, I just lost an elder who passed away. This elder, along with others, filled a small void for me. He was there after my own father died, and I realize more and more that our elders give us more of their wisdom than we may think. When I began recording, I used to let everybody I knew check out my sound and have them comment and give feedback. Over time I learned that not everyone will give you great advice or criticism. You have to trust your own sound. I'm not saying don't take advice; you don't need superstars in the industry to school you on music. Use the people in your own life and listen to their wisdom. My father used to sit me down with different music styles/cultures and break down different sounds. I appreciated his wisdom.

I had a beautiful conversation with an elder who was a fan of a Queens, New York rap artist "One Mic." This is the power of music for us. Music has definitely been my therapy for the past 24 years. I was misdiagnosed with a mood disorder and survived gang life. A lot of my music is an expression of my struggles with my past and also my successes, which gives me the ability to do what I do. Whatever your

struggles in life, use them in your music, then you'll be more authentic. The making of all my albums has been my therapy to some extent. Take care of your mental health, and know that you are not your diagnosis; you are more, and your music will help you like my music helps me. That is the purpose of this book.

When the most popular rapper at the time messages you in your Instagram and tells you "You about that music grind huh?!" and proceeds to tell you he's feeling your sound, you know you're onto something, like the rap legend from New York told me after hearing my old music. He's 1/3 of the biggest rap crew in hip hop at the time and I have his attention. I'm not a gangster, drug dealer, or pimp, obviously, but I was so influenced by their sound and delivery, and I do songwriting exceptionally well. Obviously, all my favorite rappers, DJs, and producers, legends or new legends let me know, "BIR WITNESS, YOU'RE DOPE." I was living the dream when one of the biggest DJs messages me a couple weeks later. I am getting co-signed left and right in 2020, and it feels like everything is about to take off. I'm still riding the wave but being a lot smarter.

SHADY BUSINESS

When I share with you about the shady part of the hip hop music industry, I am not speaking of any specific artist or legendary rapper, in particular, or about a Detroit, Michigan *executively produced level of shady*. I've worked with and developed my skills with famous rappers, all solid. But not everyone is gang and there are many rappers who call me family, but most are not a part of my family, and never will be. Again, there are levels to this. I've had those who, for a price, say that they will put together a video drop, they'll co-sign a song, and then showcase their Instagram stories. I'd agreed to pay them and then they decided not to do it, for some vague reason.

There have been those that have taken the money and not responded to my Instagram messages, they've refused to return my deposit or give my investment back. This is what you call shady business; the shady underbelly of the industry, people who knowingly take advantage of one's newness or those being naive. Do not let yourself be blinded by celebrity. Lessons learned. I won't drop names, but when an industry artist uses his iconic status and celebrity to make you believe he's helping you level up, be sure to trust behavior, not empty promises. The reality is that that person may be wasting your time. Believe me, it happens all the time.

Early on in my career, I had an industry rapper take months to get back to me, well after I had paid him, and it stressed me out. I learned very hard and fast not to trust these industry rappers, and you shouldn't either. You wouldn't buy a car sight unseen, right? Do your research. Learn discernment and get connected to those with integrity, such as myself. Not all will keep to their word while accepting your money. A DJ had a Spotify project in the works, so we agreed to talk business. I later found out that he lied about the details and later offered a video drop; go figure. I can't believe I went through all of that based on a lie. Don't let your hunger for fast money or clout lower your score. Then there are those that will *still* charge you a lot of money for an hour or two of their time, but getting their wisdom, truth be told, is totally worth it. I felt that way when speaking with a VP of a major record label.

PRACTICE MAKES PERFECT

My mentor told me to open up about my personal life so I could grab people into my music. All I can say is practice makes perfect because some posts worked, and some didn't get views or likes. It takes a lot to be an artist, and the man behind many big artists I call My Dream Killer (LOL), said to me, "Can you keep up?! Your music fits what everybody else is doing but can you keep up?!" Keeping up is another word for can you invest consistently? I have been investing in myself 365 days out the year for seventeen years straight. I hustled to write a book this good.

A music career takes more than Instagram and Face-book Vlogs. You can't eat in the music industry with food stamps or bad credit. You get it? Remember what I told you about DOPE music, it does not matter – well, it does matter, it's just nobody cares about your music if the rollout isn't correct. I need you to ask yourself if this is the life you want to lead. Being a star for your friends and family is cool. Thanksgiving and Christmas can make you feel really good about yourself, but I'm talking mega stardom, the level of artist that makes all the money in the music business, and gets paid for the love of it. You can see the difference between being a star at the family dinner table and a mega star who can light up a stadium. Ask yourself, are you really an entertainer? How far do you really want your journey to go?

When I was 21, I was hitting major hip hop blogs, getting thousands of plays, views, and comments. I told The Dream Killer I was ready to take it to the next level and he replied, "What's the next level? You're already doing more than most." Years later I made it even farther, got all these co-signs, and eventually things got weird. It's not about me being able to reach out to wealthy artists, producers, and DJs on social media; it's about them being able to reach out to me because they see a dedicated young artist like me investing in myself and my willingness to spend money. It's not always music or friendships; keep in mind it is still a business. I will always say to do it for the love of it, never do it just for money. Do everything yourself and forget about all the help. The money will come from your love of it and the work you put into it.

I invested over thirty thousand independently into my third album *Perfection 3*, worked on my social media for a year and a half *consistently* during the Covid-19 lockdown, and worked smart preparing for when things opened back up. I made a return to music streaming and received more awareness during the pandemic. I'm defined by my work ethic. My work ethic is stellar. Remember to do it smart, have a plan; investing in yourself is always a gamble, doing music and everything you see or hear about from me is strategic. I didn't get this far daydreaming and moving in slow motion, and like The Dream Killer was always trying to remind me, I'm closer to the finish line than most.

Coming from experience I can't say it enough. I suggest you do things yourself, invest what you can, and get busy on social media, multiple platforms. Gain a following through real networking and putting in overtime. Do not waste time fantasizing about being an overnight celebrity. All in all, social media works, and you should be getting active. All it takes is one song on Tik-Tok, a viral post on Instagram, the right video upload on YouTube, and some Facebook promo and you can blow up! Well, that's if your song is a certified hit.

Another group of people with integrity in this business is run by a successful songwriter. You can email me at christvision1111@gmail.com for more information. I have talked to an executive there many times in Zoom meetings with the label, and even via email, and he has been very helpful. I recommend any artist, producer, or just about anybody interested in the music industry to look into this business. I've traded mental health stories with a *Forbes 30 under 30* who's written for major artist, and she requested a verse from me via Instagram. Good people, good music, supportive community, and an all-around great network. She recognized I was qualified to lead. Invest in yourself properly!! I've done business with all my childhood heroes. The work with these major artists was done in less than two years, all due to my work ethic and, secondarily, money. Everyone mentioned adds value to my name. Now when it comes to not spending but making money., I've worked with many Grammy winning producers and engineers and successful PUBLISHING companies. I signed licensing deals under many producers and publishing companies as a songwriter and producer. This opportunity happened because I cared about quality production, great engineering, and being a great rapper. My music has been receiving licensing money all four quarters of the year for over a decade now. Network, build, reach out to people that can make things happen. This is the business of music. Whether you like doing business or not, nothing will get done if you don't have your money right and your business straight. If you really want to push forward, get management. Not everyone can do what I've done.

WHAT'S YOUR SOUND?

"Bir Witness has an authentic style with a broad diversity. Introspective bars and stylistic flows blend to bring you his unique brand of delivery. No matter the beat you can count on all killer and no filler with Bir." - Indie label executive

Maybe you have some producers in mind or maybe you need to find some. Either way we need to figure out your sound for your album. You need the beats first, so you can begin to write and properly craft your individual sound. It's all about vocal presence, flow, and delivery laid over quality production. An incredible Boston producer on a successful West Coast production team dropped some gems when we were on the phone for two hours. He said I should listen to my favorite records, whatever I liked, and take from that sound and make it my own. He told me that in the rap game, like the professional basketball league, not everybody makes it, no matter how skilled they are. He shared about his artist he locked in to work with, a Detroit Michigan famous artist, did a group project on a major label and was dressing like he wasn't signed to a major label. Dude, you made it, your style should match your sound fashion, haircut, everything!! He said his legendary Compton label owner would insult producers if a beat didn't sound like his famous protégés always requesting beats. He would say, "My Detroit artist would never rap on that, my Long Beach, California artist would say that's trash, my really successful New York artist wouldn't even pass that to his supergroup." He said, "Make an album if that's your thing, but it's not necessary. I say all you need is a dope single and some money to invest in the outcome because you can be successful if you make the investment in yourself." I'm well over $100,000 invested since I started. The music business is not the same and will always change. Define your own success. We're creating this album because you are a true artist.

I was also told by a legendary artist popularly known for his work with the biggest rapper out of the West, "Put the pen to the paper and write that real." He even said he would sign me if he wasn't so busy with himself and his other artists. That was a big accomplishment, knowing I grew up listening to this very artist in high school. Try putting headphones on and falling asleep to the thought of making a classic album, I was told by another ghostwriter for a Compton super producer, during the gangster rap era. I didn't find the industry, the industry found me. I've never felt like I didn't make it or didn't belong, because I was always welcome. Even before I started investing in myself, I was able to establish more of a relationship with wealthy artists and producers.

You need to put in lyrical exercise and really work your creative muscles. Let's get in the studio and really work, enough of the talking. You should have your producers, something written, and more direction than you initially started with. Let's start!! From the top, try different deliveries, try tapping into a different energy. Your voice will change the more you put into it, but keep going in. Let's try different beats. What have you got written about this?! How 'bout this beat?! We'll be doing this for hours, so stay focused. Let's discover your sound. I repeated a lyrical bar over fifty times to get the right cadence when I worked on *Perfection*.

I started out delivering my verses so many times to get where I'm at now with my delivery. I've always been around so many perfectionists and I've been recording music for so long, I have honed my craft, and I've developed my sound and since redefined my sound. I'm very consistent; it's not easy. Repetition, practice, and determination will define you as an artist in the studio, on stage, and in front of the camera. Finding your unique sound will become effortless and redefining that sound will come naturally, in time. I see you're serious, so let's make a hit!

SONG STRUCTURE

"When I first started working with Bir Witness, I instantly knew he had talent and that he was different from other MCs. He lives in Boston, but he is connected with West Coast music. Initially, he had talent and could write a mean 16 but his song structure wasn't quite in place just yet. His bars came from the heart, and he wasn't afraid to talk about real topics that he was experiencing in his life, such as mental health.

"As we began to work more and more, I saw immediate progression. He wanted the energy of today's rap but with the bars and concepts of late 90's and early 2000 era rappers. We decided to mix his records analog on the SSL board to give it a classic feel.

Through hard work and dedication, his songwriting ability just got better and better. He grew from a rapper with a hot 16 to an artist who could write dope records from start to finish. Some artists never make it to that point, but he made the transition. When you hear Bir Witness music you won't get a bunch of bull that doesn't make sense. You are going to get a well thought out and clever record with a strong delivery and great mic presence." - Westcoast Engineer/Producer for Bir Witness

"Bir Witness is a multi-dimensional artist in the sense that he has music for any mood or emotion. He is the type of artist that can successfully create dynamic art to any style of production, and he displays vivid lyricism with a cunning flow to match." - Canadian Producer for Bir Witness

Let's write! Start with a few words for the intro. You can either go with an eight-bar hook or a sixteen-bar verse after the intro. Count 1, 2, 3, 4…1, 2, 3, 4; every 4 is one bar. Yes, it takes work to put a song together. Nowadays I just write in song structure without counting bars, but when you're just starting out, you have to count the bars. So, it goes four bar intro, 16 bar verse, eight bar hook, 16 bar verse, repeat hook, and four bar outros. That is what we call song structure. The formula that everyone is used to so follow the blueprint every successful artist has used, and you will have a radio hit to launch your album.

SONGWRITING

"He's a visionary, clever with rhyme skills, and is different from a lot of artists that simply sound the same. His diverse and unique way he puts songs together, definitely separates him from the rest." – My famous uncle in California

I first started songwriting at the age of fifteen and never stopped learning, even after being considered great at the age of twenty; when I finished my first album, I signed a licensing deal. What can I say, I'm a natural, and my ability to adapt to the mood, melody, and vibe makes me a top hip hop songwriter in New England. Practice makes perfect, so I encourage you to write constantly and study the classics.

I've submitted my music to labels and have been considered by some of my favorite artists to write for their companies, and even though I can write for others I prefer writing for myself. Music is therapy for me, and a majority of artists I speak to say their music catalog is directly connected to their heart. You'll go much farther on this journey if you "Write the Real," whatever that means to you. I know this is for YOU because you too can bounce back like Bir Witness. The industry can be cruel. I put GOD first in my music career and automatically I've seen a greater win on this journey. Write like you're writing a book and stay dedicated, focus, learn from these pages, really pay close attention. Do it for the love, never for the money, and always stay humble; you can miss an opportunity forgetting who provided it, the *Ultimate* Executive Producer.

MAKE SURE YOU HAVE A GREAT ENGINEER

Here are a few of my mine and what they shared about me:

"I always enjoy it when I see Kabir hitting my line. I know he's ready to go and just needs me to put the finishing touches on his recordings. A great engineer is crucial in helping an artist get a competitive sound, as well of taking care of issues that only an engineer may be aware of."

- Engineer in Atlanta, Georgia

"Bir Witness, what can I say...He is probably one of the hardest working and most consistent artists I have worked with. I first met him while working on his record 'Come See Bout Me.'. He had reached out to an artist and from there we started our long-standing working relationship. I guess what makes him consistent is the fact that he really prepares and plans out every move he makes when it comes to creating and releasing his music. When I was mixing 'Come See Bout Me' for his album he let me know that I could take my time on it because he had two albums already complete that were set to release before the one I was currently working on. That showed me right there how much planning goes into his work."

-Audio Engineer in Boston, Massachusetts

I was always told a bad mix reflects an amateur artist and I refuse to put my name on an album mixed poorly, but we don't have to worry about that. The best advice I can give you is similar to the advice given about finding your sound. Listen to your favorite albums and pay attention to how they are mixed and mastered. Send your engineer a few samples; these are called *Reference Tracks*. You don't have to settle for just anybody and you don't have to be stingy. Invest in yourself and watch your album turn into what you are used to hearing on the radio. Your vocal tone, your delivery, your energy should all be captured in the *Mix and Master*.

Sometimes records have to be mixed fifty times to really get it right. The more records the better; it will really help with the creative process between a recording artist and music engineer. You need to develop that sixth sense with your engineer to go from wanting to make a classic to actually making a classic.

THE MIXTAPE

"Mixtapes are very important to hip hop. The mixtape gives the artist an opportunity to showcase their skill in preparation of a debut album. Mixtapes also allow the artist to bypass sample clearance, giving them a better opportunity to showcase their talent over beats that are already popular. This is key for an upcoming artist. For instance, an artist will use the instrumental from a top charting song that's already out and well known, and even if the artist is unknown the instrumental will give them a better opportunity to be heard. Mixtapes also give record labels the opportunity to reevaluate talent and artists the opportunity to put out music with label support. Mixtapes are an effective tool for artists."

– Producer from California

I promise you, original beats are the best way to move in today's climate of mixtapes. You won't make an impact using industry beats. Treat your mixtape like an album. It's time to show off your lyrical skills, straight to the point, great music. A mixtape sets the tone; if it's really great, you just have to tap into that creative power and never stop investing good coin in beats and writing classic material. Make sure just like your great album, you apply the same blueprint to your mixtape. Make anthems, bring the beast out, show your teeth! Promote your mixtape like it's an album release. Have a great title and great artwork. Study your favorite mixtapes, music, titles, and how they handle promotion. My dad always told me, "The listener needs a sample of your music before they buy your album and a mixtape is the album before the official album, so you can still dominate a playlist."

"Between the 1990's & early 2000's mixtapes were an essential part of an upcoming artist's career. A mixtape was really an artist's unofficial first album or a demo of sorts for the streets before the world was in tune with an artist in the music business. While the impact of the mixtape may have died down, soon after the internet blogs, and now playlisting, have allowed artists to still make their mark on the game."

– DJ/promoter from Philadelphia

STAY ACTIVE ON SOCIAL MEDIA AND INVEST IN SELF

If you want to do business with people on the level you admire, you must put your money up. Talent can get you in the door, but work ethic will buy you the building. Save your coins and build a website after you build your business up with a lot of work put forth. Bring the people to you. You can't make money off the job if you don't buy the materials first, and you don't buy materials for a job you can't sell. I didn't learn that in the music industry. I learned that from working with my father, a carpenter, and applied the same principles to the music industry. To me, investing in yourself shows how dedicated you are about your craft and how much it means to you. By doing so that makes other people want to invest and contribute to your movement - Imagine your favorite rapper of all time in a multi-million-dollar studio, lighting up a cigar to your music while bobbing his head to every word. Go on my official artist channel on YouTube. My favorite rapper from New York told me this book idea was dope. I know music and I know how to produce, write a song, record, mix and master to perfection. Pay attention! Let's make a hit and make some money while we're at it. I'm always focused in the studio so when you come in here make sure you're ready to work and listen carefully to my instructions so I can guide you to success. Imagine I'm in the studio with you as you read this book. Just do what an artist does and let me produce. Welcome to No More Lies Entertainment, the House Jesus Built.

RADIO PLAY AND STREAMING YOUR MUSIC

"'We On' is the record I heard that had me saying, 'Okay, this dude got something.' The record had the sound of the time and Bir Witness was among many artists pushing heat out of New England at the time. Always made sure to show homie love with my time on The Launchpad at Jamn945 Boston. The record stood out and was DJ friendly. Bir Witness understands how to pay it forward and show love when others show it to him. Stand up dude."

- JAMN 94.5 DJ Boston, MA

Over 300,000 streams in the last four years of music for the world, 300,000 streams in four months of Christian hip hop. I have 11 spins on the biggest radio station for hip hop in Boston and recognition as a producer of one of the hottest artists in the city. You need to conquer everything. When releasing your album, establish a network of DJs and promoters. Since the age of sixteen, I have been networking and building relationships with music industry professionals. I am 38 now, and I'm showing no sign of slowing down. Zoom calls discussing my business potential with a self-made millionaire. Three-hour building session with a billionaire's son, on the phone for two hours with a major record label executive Chopping it up with a multiplatinum producer for two hours twice in one week. I know music. I know business. I get along with everybody, never burn bridges, because we're all working towards a common goal. Your music is great, but the only way you succeed in this business is your network. Reach out to real people that can get you on streaming playlists, new release placements, and you need radio. People still listen to the radio, so connect with the DJs and get heard! If I can do it, you can do it also. Keep the faith.

MUSIC STREAMING

"Bir Witness has a tremendous catalog, and each song draws you into his world. Delivery and flow combined with descriptive tales from his perspective will have you wanting to hear more. I've worked with Bir Witness for quite some time and his dedication to his craft is unmatched. Consistent releases are what thrives in the streaming world by giving the fans what they want and need, which is music. Boston's own Bir Witness will have a great future and success with consistency and unparalleled work ethic. Make sure to listen to his I AM Bir Witness Playlist to get a glimpse of his catalog and hear what it means to be a great artist."

**- Marketing and Promotion/
Helped Artist Reach 1 million + Streams.**

MAJOR HIP HOP BLOGS

"Bir witness is a talented artist I had the pleasure of working with starting in 2010. He reached out to me in need of digital marketing services that I provided. His sound instantly caught my attention because he was an East Coast artist with an infectious West Coast-type sound and flow. In today's age of social media and easy access, Bir had no problem with investing in his career in hopes that it could potentially garner some attention to his music.

"Even when we may not have had a digital campaign to work on, I always thought it was important to keep up with him, motivated him by reaching out via text to send words of encouragement, because I believed in him that much. I'm proud to have worked with him in the past and we have a lot more history to create so we have work to do."

-A&R/Artist Management in the Music

I wasn't familiar with this type of promotion until I started working with my DJ in January 2010. These major hip hop blogs add huge value to your brand; they're basically like popular magazines of the past, putting you on the front page. This level of exposure is a *must* for any artist; it's a visual experience for the fans and if they are not familiar with you then invest in this promotion. The fans get to see and hear your music in the company of some of the greatest in the game to do it. I was *Heater of I Day* on one of the biggest blog sites at the time. I've seen thousands of plays, having been placed five times myself. I've been in online magazines, major magazine radio, on DJs' popular blogs and plenty more in my 18 years getting recognition on major blogs. You should always get familiar with the DJ. In time, your music will get so good he won't hesitate to do business with you. Contact me for more information. I'm here for you.

BE A VISUAL ARTIST

"Working with Bir has always been ill. He always brings energy and creativity to the table, and when the camera starts recording, he knows exactly what to do.'He's a dope artist in my book and his business is on point."

- Music Video Director

You need to be a visual artist in today's world of music. Instagram, Facebook, Snapchat, Tik-Tok are all visual promotional tools for your album. Get creative and get out there and let's not forget about music videos. Describe to the director how you want to look, your vision. Remember, this is your first impression, your first single, and everything needs to be on point. Stay focused; you need to give a music video shoot you're going to be proud of. Practice makes perfect on all social media and music videos. Film yourself, take pictures, buy a phone with a good camera; image is everything. Study yourself, learn from your mistakes, practice everything, meditate, say a prayer, study the greats who came before you, always soak in the game. Watch a music video by your favorite artist and apply what you vibe with from it into your visuals. Your music video is a promo for your album. This is a trailer for your unique movie. Let's get it!!

"Bir Witness came ready to work for both music video shoots we worked on. Not only was he creative on set, but he was an overall fun guy to be around. When he wasn't delivering his music to camera, he was cracking

jokes with everyone on set. When you shoot music videos it's key to have someone who knows what they're doing in front of the camera. Bir Witness did just that and more."

-Video Producer

CHRIST VISION TV IS THE FUTURE

It started with viral Christian freestyle raps and expanded into a visual channel on YouTube for everything Christ-related. As I work towards the future of Christ Vision TV, my soul smiles because this is God driven. I can't share the complete vision, but subscribe to the YouTube channel. This is going to be a trillion-dollar enterprise, so stay tuned. It's God over money, and God provides many fruits for people who serve His kingdom. I want to spread peace like the Prince of Peace according to scripture in Jesus' Name.

MAKING AN ALBUM

Are you ready to create a masterpiece? What's
this album about? First, you need a theme to create a
well-rounded album from start to finish, and when you
start feeling the music, let's figure out your theme songs,
also popularly known as singles. Are you telling a story?
Is there a recurring message in your music? Is it Christian
rap, gangsta rap, or somewhere in between? I'm going to
tell you this right now; if it isn't part of your story, don't
use it as your theme. It comes off fake; keep it real. Pull
from experience to create your masterpiece. Listeners
want to hear real voices with true-to-life experiences. No
one wins being fake and phony. Longevity in music Is
only acquired when your actions meet your words. So be
you, the real you, both in and out of the Booth, because

you will be tested.

Make sure to tell your true story over quality production because there are many people in this world that need to hear it and hear it right. It's not hard to make good music. a lot of people make good music; you need the whole artist package. Even good music can just sound outdated if you wait too long to put it out, so keep it original, and fresh, and be You! I like artists that rap from the heart. I like substance. So be your true authentic self. I can't stress that enough.

I executive produced an album entitled *Crazy World* where I dealt with topics on mental health. I was right on time with that one, really capturing experiences I've been through with prescription pills, hospitals, and doctors. Now, think of your experiences and create a theme park of sorts around them, and you will be formulating a masterpiece. Every song is a ride, an experience for the next adventure. Some rides go fast, some rides go slow, but keep a balance where you want the listener to go! The production is the atmosphere you want the vocals and vocal tone to live in, to paint the picture, and amaze the eyes through sound while opening the ears. Make sure every word is clear.

Relax your mind and concentrate; don't force the

outcome. The theme is every scene; it feels like a dream sometimes, a nightmare at other times. I need you to focus; if you don't have a theme bring the listener nearby. Your theme should excite listeners from ear to ear. These are not song lyrics, lol, I just want to keep your attention on the executive producer.

You need great producers, not beat makers but experts at putting a hit record together. I trust every producer and engineer who spoke about me in my book. Work with them and thank me later. Music is not supposed to sound complicated, but the work can be very frustrating in the beginning. I wanted to quit a lot in the early stages and during difficult times. My DJ at the time always told me to keep recording, keep dropping mixtapes, albums, singles, music videos, and flood the market. To do that, I needed to discover my sound and who my go-to producers were. You might have one or two in mind; just make sure your business is straight. In the vast ocean of producers, the small fish make beats just as good, if not better than, the big fish can, so go and search online for your HIT - boy. Nowadays, superstars get popular on social media, and it's just as easy to find a so-called *Super Producer* online too. You are now the record label; you just need a laptop and a smartphone. Now that you realize you can run your own business, keep a stellar work ethic, establish yourself with some great producers, know that you deserve it, and you're on the path to being a great songwriter.

Let's listen to all the music we've created. I'm really feeling the beats, great choice of producers. The order of the songs should complement each other and showcase your best work. You always want the listener to hear your best foot forward and a constant curated song order that carries one mood to the next. Think of your album like a movie, pulling the audience in with every line, every scene. In your case every rhyme, with every song. A great movie has great actors, and a great album has great features. We are creating the soundtrack to your life, and we begin the process with your first single. You're into the music; the greatness of it should be embraced with your first single.

Yes!! I am incredible at the executive producer role, and you will want to seek that same level of greatness as an artist. Let's really break it down. I'm looking for a record to set this album off! Looking for a perfect visual, very well-crafted, love song always sets the tone. Let's really think about this because you have some really catchy, infectious records on this album.

What do you think? I'm here to give directions but

you're the artist, so paint me a picture. These songs are coming from your head, your vision, and now that your mind is clear, you can make a sound decision about your journey. We will give it another listen. Always plan on playing the music for others. Not for man's approval, but what speaks to your spirit. Excitement fuels the culture and will fuel you in your creative, beast mode. Yes, you are creating a movie through sound, and the world pays attention if it's exciting and people can relate. Do you have your first single?

My studio engineer friend once told me about a popular New York rapper that released a platinum single to the masses and his album *still* wasn't finished. With all the excitement and the hype, this rapper was able to write from a winning perspective because the whole world was waiting for his album. You can do the same, just focus on how well your first single is doing.

"I've known Bir Witness for a long time and watched him grow from a young, enthusiastic kid with a lot of ideas and creative energy into the artist you see today. He's spent the last eighteen years honing his craft, bringing his vision into focus, and you can see that growth in his body of work. I've worked with artists of all genres at all levels- and Bir Witness has a creative drive and work ethic most can only aspire to."

- My first engineer

Here is some of the feedback that you will hear when working with different producers. You also will learn to listen to your tracks and keep in mind what needs to be done; you'll develop an ear for it. If you don't hear it directly, your executive producer will. "Harder hitting drums, more bass, more instruments, I need this tracked out, your vocals are too low, wait…Now your vocals are too high. Do the first verse over, redo the hook. Let's hear the recording back. How do you feel about the music, because this doesn't scream *masterpiece*. We need more records. This album is missing important song topics. Too many tracks with the same type of production."

I understand you are your mom's favorite rapper and she loves your voice, but come on, we need to make something the hip hop culture will enjoy. I'm not trying to be too hard on you but if I have to, I will. Sugar-coating does us both a disservice. To perfect this album, your single needs to be great out the gate, if the proper work is put into it. A lot of people are excited and on your side. Let's just keep putting in the work. It's crunch time, and this is how we talk during the finishing process. Don't take it personally; it's part of the work in music.

After putting in the hard work, my debut album *Perfection* got me a music licensing deal shortly after it was released, as mentioned earlier, by a Grammy-winning publishing company. I've been getting royalty checks off my first album, *Perfection*, for the past fourteen years.

The first song I recorded for the album was "In My Hood," featuring a singer/songwriter. You always need a great feature to compliment your skill set. The beat was simple; however, our vocals really brought it to life. Great engineering for that record, and we recorded the vocals very quickly; the flow was organic and easy. My verses were dark and grimy, just like the beat, so it was a perfect match. I was describing my street mentality, my experience around my neighborhood; being twenty and fighting to make it to twenty-one. The singer gave me a classic hook - very menacing, very West Coast, and just all-around genius.

I recorded the second track, "Caught Up" shortly after "In My Hood." This record also features a singer, used the same engineer, a different producer, and the beat is very musical. The verses describe how I felt after finding out my best friend got shot in the head and survived. The singer really captured the emotion of my verses through the hook. If the *formula* works, keep using it. A great singer, a great rapper, a great producer, and a great engineer will always win. No need to reinvent the wheel.

109

Let's talk about my first single, "Hustle Hard." When I first heard the beat, it was this insane loop, and I just fell in love with it. I invested in myself and purchased the beat. I took my time writing the verses, and every day after I got off work, me and the producer kept recording different vocal takes to find my sound. Man! Listen! When we found my sound, I took off! I had much more confidence, and I went out fearless and performed live, felt unstoppable, even in New York. The whole world just opened up to me and I fell in love, all over again, with the work.

My producer was also an engineer, so making records with him had a one-stop shop vibe. If possible, sit with your producer, sit with your engineer, and get involved with the work, all aspects. On *Perfection*, I was present for almost everything - from the additional production, structure of songs, recording with the producer or engineer, almost everything. "Knowledge of Self," "Train of Thought," and "Get-a-Way" all used the same formula as "Hustle Hard." We took our time, figured out my sound, and ran with it.

The theme of *Perfection* is my life story, from 1986 to age twenty-one. I reached the age of twenty-one and for me that was a huge accomplishment, considering everything I'd been through. For a young African American man, I survived a lot of the stereotypical, and not so common, pitfalls. Every track gives you a different situation, a different scenario, that plays out like a movie. A successful rapper from Atlanta told me I know how to tell my own story and he gets it. He said he understands what I'm trying to do after hearing "That's Boston." "So Tired" then went viral on Spotify. Very proud of that record. During the recording of Perfection my father was very sick. His support for my music was unmatched and unwavering.

While I was visiting him in the hospital, I wrote the record "So Tired" and it broke down how his getting worse was affecting me personally, and the whole family. My father and mother both cried when they heard "So Tired;" it was beautiful, powerful.

Perfection vibes in the college days where I met another great engineer who worked with me every day nonstop, perfecting my craft. So, if I wasn't in class, I would be writing, practicing, always going strong. Listen to me: if you really want it, you CAN have it, but you have to do the work to get the results.

"Truly Amazing" was another single, and it was a professionally shot music video by LTD FILMS. The VP

of a major label told me, "I know how to pick singles."
You're a visual artist. While watching "Truly Amazing," I
have to say you must be a visual artist to sell your music
online. Know yourself as an artist because it will show
in your music videos. The same way you have to find
your sound, you have to find yourself and know how to
showcase yourself visually. What helped me most was a
lot of studio sessions and doing shows all year round, the
feedback and constructive advice. By the time I shot my
first music video, I recognized everything was the Lord's
grace and timing, and I had gratefully begun living my
dream.

ALBUM ARTWORK

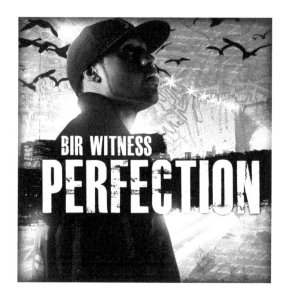

"Good artwork is legit the icing on the cake, It's the definition of that project and pretty much a vision of 'What' you were thinking and feeling during the process."

– Graphic artist from Harlem, New York

This is important. Now that the album is done, we need artwork, and not just *any* graphic designer; you need someone good. You'll need to find a designer that can *match* your vision, your energy. My graphic designer was located in Amsterdam when I started and now she's my wife and she is Holy Spirit led. You don't need to go that far, but the Internet does make it easy to go outside the boundaries of the USA for artwork and many other things. I suggest searching through Instagram; start there and just do the work, do your research. Communication is key when putting together your artwork. Let the graphic designer hear the album and speak about your vision, clearly, and your album cover will be classic. You found a great graphic designer, didn't you? It does take practice.

Remember to invest in yourself. Pay for quality because your album is going to be incredible. On my first album *Perfection,* the artwork was from the graphic designer in Amsterdam. He really took it to another level. A professional photographer, a great graphic designer, and a vision to match the cover with the music. We did just that and everything turned out classic.

"Where do I even start. I've been working with Bir Witness for more than ten years now. I was fifteen years old when I started, and he was one of the first artists I did business with. I'm 26 now and he's the only artist that really stuck with me as a client through all these years. I've really been through a lot all these years with personal problems like mental health issues and Bir Witness always respected that and that's one of the things I really appreciate about him. He also gave me a lot of freedom with the artwork, which was great for me also as an artist.

"I can say I really feel like I'm part of the Money and a Dream family. Bir Witness is a pure artist with amazing lyrics, and I'm glad he stayed true to himself and didn't sell out like a lot of other artists."

-Amsterdam Graphic Designer

"In my frame of mind, he seems to me as a reflection of a legend who managed to win an appreciable reputation and a remarkable figure of fame."

- Tattoo Artist/Graphic Designer

MERCHANDISE

Every artist needs merchandise. Fans love merchandise. I created an online store on *Shopify,* selling custom clothing, and the fans showed their support. All my designs, representing my music, SOLD OUT quickly because I was strategical. I posted pics of fans wearing my merch. I wore my merch in music videos, studio sessions, and photoshoots. Artists make most of their money off merchandise and touring. Do good work with a good attitude and you'll get results. The popularity will bring more and more attention but know it's a full-time job to sustain it, to keep touring, and to keep the merch selling out.

Always keep a positive attitude and represent your brand with quality merchandise. I was always into fashion and looking my best, so I brought that same standard into my clothing. It felt good to see my fans wear my clothes, and to see an order come through is great. Not to mention, I'm making money doing what I love all aspects of, and icing on the cake. Combining the elements of hip hop and your branding, mesh together when pushing a new album. I don't want to spend too much time on this topic because we need to finish your album; worry about the merch business later. A good site is Bandcamp for all your merch needs; start a label on there after reading this book! My wife and I run a customized clothing company called Power Line Clothing. She started a few years back, it's very successful and has helped us fuel ourselves to create merch for our record label.

HAVING A MANAGER

"Management is definitely important, but just as important is giving management something to manage. When looking for opportunities for an artist, the other party wants to know what the artist is bringing to the table. It's just business, and with any business you look at the rate of return. So, what does the other party get besides the artist's talent? Talent is everywhere today. Make sure you have something more than just talent to sell.

"Even though they are constantly thinking about the next step, a management company can also deal with daily operations for the artist. They are the voice of the artist, representing them in front of industry professionals. Through these connections, the manager can help you find many opportunities. These may include gig offers, music blogs, asking to feature the artist, and other industry attention as previously mentioned. As the voice of the artist, it is important for the manager and artist to have a positive relationship and be on the same wavelength. This will ensure the right decisions will be made, with no confusion or conflict. It is hard to develop as an artist if your manager does not understand your ambitions, so it is important to bond and have a good relationship. In the end, this will affect the health of your career as an artist.

"A manager's primary role is to be the buffer between the artist and all business entities, including the record label, other artists, show promoters, producers, sponsors, and all people who want to make money with the artist. A good manager will make sure that an artist never has to handle prices or even discuss the business with anyone except the manager. A manager's role is to allow the artist to focus on the music by taking care of all the other tasks for the artist. Managers will also negotiate contracts and try to secure new business for the artist. Artists always want to be viewed in a positive light. For instance, your artist charges $2500 per feature and the person trying to purchase the feature has $1500 dollars. It's not the artist's job to tell the purchaser that's not enough money; it's the manager's role to do that. A normal day for a manager would be to consult with the artist and figure out the goals they want to achieve for that day and for their career, then help the artist achieve that. But a good manager will go above and beyond to find new revenue streams for that artist along with helping to execute the artist's vision." – Music industry manager

I've never had a manager. I'm a hard-working artist; I'm always working so much. I love managing myself. I've learned to trust myself, but I also keep a lot of professionals in the music business busy too. I just keep investing in myself, on all levels, with plenty of trophies. That's what I call all my wins. I've signed deals, booked shows, opened up for celebrities, made major connections, made business agreements, and put other artists ON, one after the other. It's your choice on what is best for you in the management business.

PERFORMING AN ALBUM LIVE

"Bir Witness comes on stage with a gritty street aura, but also combined with a welcoming warmth and attitude that is sure to captivate the audience. By mixing harsh street tales with a quirky and sometimes sinister attitude, Bir has something for everyone. When Bir performs you can feel a sense of urgency in the air which leaves you wondering what he's going to say next. Whether he's vibing with the audience or talking about personal struggles, Bir is able to blend a certain vulnerability with a strong, soldier-like drive which allows fans of all walks of life to relate to his music."

After I finished my first single, I started performing live. My confidence went through the roof because I did some next-level music with a producer who went on to produce and mix for a *successful artist from Worchester, Massachusetts*. I've opened for celebrities, headlined clubs, and performed in Brooklyn twice, all at the age of 21. I've been doing shows since. The motivation and hunger is the same; my first single, the music, the feedback, the excitement around the music, is something to be shared with others. So, get out there and embrace it, live it, and show your talent. Continue to be yourself. Throw a concert and bring your album to life.

After I released *Perfection*. I put together a concert that summer. "I DO SHOWS LIKE I'M ON TOUR." Everyone got paid and my loyal fans really enjoyed the show. Since I was 21, I've always had a *Hype Man*. But I also performed more shows alone. Biblically pray, practice, and execute. Sometimes promoters want you to pay them to perform your own music, but that wasn't my thing. There are plenty of shows you can get booked and set up for yourself, by yourself, and for your crew too.

Seek out those opportunities; that will look good for your image, and it shows. Get the support of your fans and soon you may open up for celebrities and sell tickets.

To me, the recording process is great and exciting. but the performance side is for the people, and solidifies your connection with them. Both performing and recording are very therapeutic, but something about performing live is just euphoric. When the energy is right, there's nothing like it.

"As for the artistic aspect of performing live, this is where you separate the EMCEES from the RAPPERS. I came up on cats who took it seriously, so I do the same. No rapping over vocals, keep that breath control right, rhyme with clarity and whether it's five or 5,000 people, you tear that stage DOWN! Another aspect that's overlooked and crucial is the DJ. Your DJ can literally make or break your performance, so chemistry with him or her is vital."

– Artist from Haverhill, Massachusetts

LICENSING DEALS AND ROYALTY CHECKS

I met a man that changed my life when it came to licensing and royalties in music. He signed me to a licensing deal at the age of twenty-one and I got my first royalty check two years later. He still sends me royalties in check form. I'm thirty-eight now and still receiving them every year. I also get royalties in check form from my own publishing company, and this has been going on for over a decade. I've been paid all four quarters of the year consistently for years now. As a music composer, I truly believe it is important to understand how music royalties and publishing work in the music industry.

Here is some general information:

When it comes to collecting music royalties, there are two equal shares: the publisher's share which is 50%, and the songwriter's share which is also 50%. Music publishers collect the publisher's share and the performance rights organizations (PRO's) such as BMI, ASCAP or SESAC pay the royalties to the songwriter(s) directly.

"Music publishing is simply the collection and payment of royalties from songs that have been used. Music publishers typically collect all the music publishing royalties on behalf of the songwriter. The publisher then takes a cut in exchange for administration services. The songwriter's royalties, which is the other share, is collected by the PROs on behalf of the songwriter. These royalties are Performance royalties, mechanical royalties and synchronization royalties."

– Music publisher

ALBUM DISTRIBUTION & RECORD DEALS

"Bir Witness is more than a catchy name; Bir witness came to change the game. He uses a dope rhyme pattern to deliver hard hitting bars. In a time where lyrics are scarce, Bir Witness continually delivers hit after hit. He has endless talent and is one of the premier lyricists in hip hop today."

– Famous rapper from Orange County, California

I've been signed to four different distribution deals. My first deal was a great one. I learned a lot about distribution deals and how they work and this prepared me for how to handle and what to look for with the other three. My first deal had a direction and a natural flow and was executed properly. We released an EP I wrote during my two weeks' stay in India. My second distribution deal was signing to a label. I was signed as an artist to a West Coast label. The CEO started this label when he was signed to a Detroit, Michigan legend in hip hop. I passed my album in, and the CEO loved It! The album was *Perfection 3.* I left the label, and my third distribution deal was perfect, because I had much more control than I had with the other two.

I left the third deal and I'm currently releasing music with my wife through our ministry No More Lies Entertainment. When your album is finished, you could sign a distribution deal or do it all yourself.

My first album, *Perfection*, is still making me money after all these years, and this isn't something only I can do; you can network and have these same opportunities or even better. Reach out and grab these opportunities! You may be one conversation away, with the right publishing company, from getting PAID! You need to meet the people that make money with music. You need to travel, meet and greet, introduce yourself. Don't be afraid to make money and don't be afraid to spend money. Remember, YOU are the director too, and I am just motivating you to keep writing your script and read Bible scripture so you too can get baptized and navigate through the Holy Spirit. You too can reap the benefits of collecting royalty checks for the rest of your life, like me, from your first album. You got this, and Jesus got you!!

ABOUT KABIR "BIR WITNESS" JAMAL

A Child of God who does music for the Kingdom of God to strengthen faith and obedience, Bir Witness has done music business with many major and indie artists, producers, and engineers. He knows the right sound and the right frequencies to create a great record. He'll lead you and your team on a journey to success. He's a visionary. His music has been on XXL, NBC, CBS, Sony Music, Universal Music Group, NBA TV, NBA Inside Stuff, Atlanta's Streetz 94.5 and Boston's JAMN 94.5. He's not afraid to play his music for anyone if given the opportunity. His ups and downs define his catalog of releases on streaming services everywhere.

Nomoreliesentertainment.bandcamp.com

Instagram: @iambirwitness X: @birwitness

Facebook.com/birwitness

Milton Keynes UK
Ingram Content Group UK Ltd.
UKHW020249260424
441678UK00005B/57